MW01534122

SAFEGUARD

Real Self-Defense for a Changing World

SAFEGUARD

Real Self-Defense for a Changing World

CONTRIBUTING AUTHORS:
TROY AUMAN
TOM BURT
VINCENT-MARCO DUCHETTA
JUSTIN EVERMAN
JIM HAMMONS
LEONARDO LECHUGA
BRETT LECHTENBERG
MOLOTOV MITCHELL

EDITORS:
ALEX CHANGHO & MICHAEL CUDDYER

SAFEGUARD
Real Self-Defense for a Changing World

Copyright © 2016 Alex Changho

All Rights Reserved. No part of this publication may be reproduced in any form or by any means, including scanning, photocopying, or otherwise without prior written permission of the copyright holder.

DEDICATION

The country where I live, the United States of America, is one of the safest countries in the world.

And it's because of a culture of respect and awareness, as well as people who protect us from those who choose to be hurtful, both domestically and internationally.

This is dedicated to those folks who dedicate their lives to protect others. The military, the police, law enforcement, as well as everyone out there educating the public about safety, including private citizens and businesses.

It is together that we can make our world a safer place.

TABLE OF CONTENTS

INTRODUCTION: USING THIS BOOK

BY ALEX CHANGHO
CARY, NORTH CAROLINA

Safety.

We're taught this from the time we are little kids. Wear your seatbelt, look both ways before crossing the street, and don't play with matches.

But when it comes to safety involving another human being, the instructions that kids are taught are not as universal.

If a child is dealing with someone trying to hurt them, one parent may say "walk away," while the other parent says "hit them back."

And this continues as a child grows up into an adult.

The idea for *Safeguard* came while I was publishing Volume 3 of *BULLYPROOF: Unleash the Hero Inside Your Kid.* While most bullying today comes in forms that are more emotional than physical (cyber bullying, teasing, etc), as adults the threats can become more hands-on.

What is real, true self-defense? That is the question that came to my mind. There are lots of ways to defend yourself... what would the experts say?

We've brought together eight experts in self-defense. They all have martial arts backgrounds and most cross train in other forms of personal protection, including firearms.

Safeguard is meant to give a no-nonsense look at self-defense and why it is so vital today to have a familiarity, for the sake of oneself and their loved ones.

Chances are, you picked up this book because you met one of the featured authors. Read their chapter first. If it resonates with you, I'd recommend you explore more with them about their particular art of self-defense. If not, read on. But I promise you: you will *not* learn self-defense from reading a book. You *will* learn self-defense by training consistently, over a duration of time, with an expert.

Whether you work with someone you found on your own, or with one of the eight featured experts, you'll find that you become stronger and more confident that you can take care of yourself.

Alex Changho is a lifestyle and business coach. With almost two decades of experience leading and motivating others, and running a business, he helps business owners integrate their life's mission and career with their personal side of their life.

Alex is the founder of BULLYPROOF America, a non-profit with the mission of helping local communities educate families about bullying and help create confident kids.

An accomplished speaker and presenter, Alex is a Master NLP Practitioner and Trainer, Senior Leader with Anthony Robbins, and Master Strengths Coach.

Alex lives in North Carolina with his cat Bert.

For more information, visit www.alexchangho.com.

CHAPTER 1:
THE REALITY OF SELF-DEFENSE

BY JUSTIN EVERMAN
RICHARDSON, TEXAS

When we hear the word "safety" it conjures up thoughts ranging from personal defense to home defense, to that of national security and everything in between. That said; today I'd like to set our focus to personal safety. By personal safety we of course mean we will be talking about of self-defense related topics. This has been near and dear to my heart for most of my life and it's truly an honor to be able to share my passion for this training with the world.

I've been fortunate in that I've had both a number of traditional and non-traditional forms of self-defense training throughout the course of my life.

For me, the exposure to traditional martial arts came at a young age as a way to cope with being bullied in school. While there were some great takeaways from that type of training, I also realized there were some big disconnects between what was being taught and what was happening to me in real life. That eventually led me down a path that would span a lifetime of research and development which ultimately culminated with me creating systems that focused on real world self-defense scenarios and situations. Over the years, I've worked diligently to become an expert at effectively conveying these solutions to others so they too can stay safe. My training system, A.C.W.A. Combatives, focuses on reality based self-defense as well as the creation of the proper mindset to be able to dynamically problem solve and persevere. We often say our #1 goal is "to get you home safe at night".

The Necessity of Self-Defense

As with all things in this world, "opinions may vary" and this is certainly true as it applies to the differing viewpoints on the importance of self-defense. One camp believes that learning to protect oneself and their loved ones isn't all that important. More likely than not, they have never personally been subject to violence at the hands of another and think this type of thing "only happens to other people". They place faith in conventional security and laws to protect them, or even worse, they turn a blind eye to the world around them choosing ignorance and denial over reality and solutions. Don't get me wrong, there is nothing wrong with seeing the good in those around you, but know that the world is not all puppy dogs and unicorns, there are wolves among us, so it's best to be prepared.

Self-defense training gives you a plan of action to fall back on when it matters most. It's like having a fire extinguisher in your home just in case something happens. If you have a small fire in the kitchen, you can grab said extinguisher and eliminate the threat before it spreads. If you don't have a fire extinguisher right when you need it, then the fire can spread, causing much more damage (which could have been avoided with some foresight). Self-defense is like that, it's something everyone should have access to at a moment's notice, just in case. As the old adage goes, it's better to have and not need than to need and not have.

We look at self-defense as tool, just like the fire extinguisher, it helps us solve a problem in an expedient fashion. When there is no fire, the fire extinguisher is out of sight, concealed from view, but ever ready should the situation call for it; the same general rules can apply to personal defense. I don't want to teach people to be paranoid, or think that someone is waiting to attack them around every corner, but at the same time, I don't want people to walk around with blinders on either. So while some people may not see self-defense as a necessity because they only want to focus on the good, I think it's important to realize that evil is real and simply pretending it doesn't exist is not an effective means of personal defense. Ignoring this fact is like ignoring a fire burning right next to you, you're eventually going to get burned.

With that said, perhaps you still don't think your own safety is a priority, but what if I asked you to consider what you could, or would, do to protect your family, your wife, your children, or other people you care about? Mention this factor and people's mindsets start to change. Realizing that you may be in a situation where you have to keep others safe is a great motivator, and one that has encouraged many people to seek out training. We will often fight harder and longer for someone else we care about than we will for ourselves because we fear losing them (fear of loss is a substantial motivator for us psychologically to take action). Thinking of others also forces us to consider how important our own safety is to those who love us. The idea of leaving a child without a father or mother is a powerful reason for people to learn more about personal protection.

Training Concerns

One of the biggest concerns that people voice when it comes to making a decision about self-defense is the risk of injury. While this is a valid concern, more often than not, it's more of a mental barrier people create for themselves as an excuse to stay in their comfort zone. Of course there are risks anytime you're learning something new, but many can be mitigated by proper instruction. Take swimming for example – when you go swimming there's an inherent risk of drowning every time you get in the water. So if someone with no experience is learning to swim you don't throw them in the deep end and hope for the best, literally letting them sink or swim. That would be a horrible experience, and even if they made it out, they'd probably never want to touch water again! Instead, what you ought to do is educate them and take small incremental steps. Maybe you start with breathing exercises, talk about the process, walk into the shallow end, and even use some kind of floatation device. From there you can progressively build up to more, but you don't start off by pushing them off a diving board in the deep end. Self-defense training works in much the same way. We start in the "shallow end" by working on easy to understand concepts and drills. Strikes and movements are done with maybe 10% speed and power so a person can get used to experiencing contact. Using pads or mitts also allows a person to process what's going on without becoming overwhelmed with the fear of injury. From here we move forward, gradually working our way to the "deep end". We increase speed, add more variables to the scenarios, train on different surfaces to simulate real world environments, and increase the confidence and skill as we go along. It's a process to go from the "shallow end" of training to the "deep end", but there's no need to worry about injury because we develop the skills needed as we go and make sure a student is ready before moving on.

Traditional vs. Reality Based Self-Defense

Let's take a bit of time now to address the differences between traditional martial arts vs. reality based self-defense. Traditional martial arts have some excellent qualities and have their place offering great health benefits, increased balance, and the opportunity for self-perfection. However, when it comes to real world applications, the traditional martial arts lack the necessary ingredients to be truly effective. In traditional martial arts classes there are lots of line drills, traditional forms or katas, and it's very organized and structured. The training essentially puts blinders on the students as they're focused only on a single target or drill. The movements are taught the same way they were created hundreds, or even thousands of years ago, and oftentimes that's the extent of it. Unfortunately, this is a far cry from our present day to day street reality so we must look for an alternative that addresses modern issues in ways that are applicable to today's problems; this brings us to the topic of reality based self-defense.

What reality based self-defense (and our A.C.W.A. Combatives program) offers, that traditional martial arts does not, is the chaos that comes with life. Reality based self-defense doesn't just train inside on mats – we make a point to utilize the parking lot, or surrounding grassy areas, to experience training in settings where you actually go during the day. We try our best to create chaotic environments that simulate places people may have to defend themselves. Sometimes we'll turn out the lights, turn up the music, and use lighting systems and lasers to create that chaos and unpredictability that solidifies what you're learning. If it works in this environment, then it will work nearly anywhere. Clothes even play a part in what we do as we don't wear traditional "Gi's" but instead wear blue jeans, t-shirts, and running shoes to simulate everyday life. We train to deal with simultaneous multiple attackers as group and gang attacks are less the exception to the rule and more and more the norm. We also train people how to respond to verbal assaults and preconflict cues in addition to physical attacks. If a person gets in your face and starts screaming, what would you do? If you've never experienced the adrenal dump that comes with this situation and what that does to you mentally and physically then you won't know how to act if it happens to you in your day to day life. Reality based self-defense is able to incorporate these types of scenarios into the training in ways that traditional martial arts just can't, and that's what gives it so much value.

The Layers of Self-Defense

When we talk about self-defense, one of the things we often refer to is the term "layers". There are various layers of protection that different trainings offer, and it's important to learn about how they all function and interlink with each other. One thing I see quite often is that people become overconfident when carrying some type of tool (read this as weapon, but we don't use that term in this way as the mind is the only weapon we have, everything else is just a tool or a force multiplier). For some people it's carrying a firearm, for others it's carrying a knife, or even a stun gun/taser, never mind what *it* is, the mindset surrounding the tool is always very similar. They feel that if they have this "thing" then they're protected, but really that's only one layer of protection. If you have one tool and rely solely on that then you're at a severe disadvantage, all your eggs are in one basket (better not trip). For example, I mentioned training how to respond if someone gets in your face and starts screaming obscenities. Are you really going to use that tool now to respond to this verbal situation? Most times it's simply not appropriate, or legal, to brandish and use a tool at the drop of a hat; the situation must determine the correct level of response. It's like saying you have a hammer, and you can use that one tool for every job in your house. In reality the hammer is great for striking a nail, not so much for cutting wires, patching a hole, or screwing something together.

Instead of having one tool that works for everything what you need to have are additional layers of protection. You have to have options to escalate and deescalate situations as needed, and to do that you have to have more tools in your toolbox. To really be safe you have to be able to have a Plan B for when Plan A breaks down, and a Plan C for when something goes wrong with Plan B. You need to realize that different situations warrant different responses, and you must have a degree of behavioral flexibility and an understanding of the force continuum in order to respond with the appropriate level of force. This is why the concept of layers is so important, training gives us options and facilitates us making the best choices possible with the information, time, and tools we have available.

When Should Training Start?

We have a wide diversity of ages active in the A.C.W.A. ranging from 3 to well over 70 years old. It's both ends of that group that generate the most questions about age appropriateness though. On one side of the coin we have parents asking what age is best to start their child learning about personal safety and self-protection. They are often concerned that the child may be too young. On the other side we also get inquiries from older generations that are afraid they've missed their opportunity to train. This is where I think our training system is pretty unique as it can help nearly everyone reach their goals.

On one end of the spectrum I have kids as young as three training. They train with their parents (mom or dad holds mitts and works with them under an instructors care and direction) to start very early learning about what to do if someone tries to hurt them with actions or even words. They learn about bullying, strangers, and the concept of personal protection; and while they'll learn less than older kids, they also have an amazing ability to act like sponges when it comes to learning natural movements and natural body mechanics. They're able to understand and even apply some of the most important core mechanics, and as they train with their parents they're developing in ways that will give them an incredible edge as they get older.

On the other end of our training spectrum are folks as old as 70+ years. You may ask what can they do, and the answer is everything that everyone else does. Because we train in reality based self-defense we're not doing anything that's really attribute based. We're not jumping, spinning, or doing anything really strenuous on the joints. We're not training Olympic athletes as that's not our focus – we're training everyday people who want to be safe in their regular lives. Our system is based around natural mechanics and motion, and because of our teaching methods we can train all ages as well as people with disabilities. So the answer to the question of when training should start, right now is the best time, regardless of your age. Everyone has the right to be safe.

Training for Men vs. Women

Just like the question of when people should begin training, I also commonly get the question about what the differences are in training men and training women. I understand why people have the question, and a lot of it comes down to societal norms as we see them. We've separated the term "women's self-defense" as if it's a separate entity, and many facilities have made lots of money by marketing specifically to this mindset. People seem to have images of women's self-defense being eye gouging and scratching, while men's self-defense means putting on gloves and striking each other in the face repetitively. This whole concept makes no sense to me. At the end of the day we're all built with the same structure – two arms, two legs, and a wobbly head. That means that while body sizes and types may differ, there is still lots of commonality in the mechanics of how we move.

So personally, when it comes to training men and women I don't really have a difference. I can see where that type of training can work in certain situation specific circumstances, but I'm not trying to teach 1000 situation specific defenses. My goal is for you to get out of every situation that comes along, building on concepts, not just memorized ideal situation only techniques (that you cannot really apply). If a women sees that she can defend herself against another woman, that's ok, but seeing that she can defend herself against a 300lb man, well that's a game changer.

Again, it all comes down to the fact that your training needs to be reality-based because in the real world you don't get to choose who's attacking you. Whether you're a man or a woman the assailant might be a person the same size as you, they might be smaller, or they might be twice your size. Training to defend yourself against whatever comes your way is the only way you become truly safe.

Things That Don't Work

We live in an age where information of any kind is readily available. Google "self-defense" and you'll be inundated with thousands of websites, articles, videos, and images of what people think are the best options out there. While some of the information is valuable, some of it is simply wrong and downright dangerous. It's not just what you find online either. Oftentimes students come to us with ideas they got from their friends or family members who "used to train" somewhere or was a "black belt" in something (but they don't know what). Unfortunately a lot of the advice, though well intentioned, does more harm than good, and in some instances is actually dangerous.

One really common thing I see, especially from women, is the idea of putting keys between your fingers as a way to defend yourself. Putting something hard between your fingers and smashing it against or jabbing it at a hard object, like a human skull, is going to damage your fingers more than damage the intended target. Think of it like this – would you put your keys between your fingers and punch the floor? Of course not, because it would hurt, or worse break your fingers! So why would you want to punch someone in the face or head like that? There are lots of mechanics here that simply work better and are much safer for you. This is why you should take the time to train with people who are skilled in what they're doing, who have tested what they teach, and can explain the why and the how that will keep you safe.

Another common and much related issue I see is people wanting to rely solely on tools for their safety. I touched on the use of guns and knives earlier, and while they definitely have their place in self-defense, they should be regarded as <u>an</u> answer, but not <u>the</u> entire answer. It's just not as easy as buying something and putting it in bag, holster, sheath, or pocket and thinking you're safe; that's wrong and can be a deadly mistake. When things go wrong in the real world, they go wrong incredibly fast. An opponent can close a 21 foot gap in less than two seconds. Now that's 21 feet, so if an opponent is closer, which they normally are, you're allowed response time drops even more. Drawing and using a gun, knife, or even keys effectively in that time is extremely difficult, if not impossible. This again brings us back to the idea of layering as you'll need to learn instinctual mechanics to protect yourself from the initial attack and then movements that provide you both the time and opportunity for tool acquisition. The lesson continues to be that you simply can't rely on just one tool to get every job done. Not every problem is a nail, and not every solution is a hammer, so be aware of the dynamics of a situation and train to respond accordingly.

Final Thoughts & Mindset

Protecting yourself and your family is something you should absolutely take as a serious priority and make time for. Training has shown time and time again to make all the difference when it comes to one's personal safety. When I say training, I mean both the mental and physical sides of self-defense. The most important thing you have in a self-defense situation is your mindset because a person with the right mindset can accomplish amazing things.

I like to give this example. Say there are two men who both have families. One of these men is an absolute jerk. He doesn't really care about his family in any meaningful way, but he trains religiously every day and has so for years. The second man has zero training other than watching some movie fight scenes, but he loves his family deeply and would do anything for them, they're his whole world. Which one of these men would be harder to deal with if their family is threatened – the one who doesn't care about his family, or the one who would do anything for them? The answer, of course, is the second man. That man will fight tooth and nail, he will do anything and everything he can and give it all he's got to defend his family because that's his mindset.

Mindset is the most important thing you can have; it will pull you through when everything else is falling apart. This is why we always start our students with an understanding of how key this principle is to their success not just in personal defense, but in every aspect of life. Once we have this foundation, we can start to layer in tactics, skills, and tools, but the foundation has to be there first. Simply put, without the foundation of the right mindset nothing else will get you to where you want to go. If you have the mentality and the knowledge that you're ready to do what you must to ensure the safety of yourself and your family, then you're in a place of power. Start with this as your foundation, because the right mindset can lead you to some amazing things.

Justin Everman is the founder of A.C.W.A: Academy of Combative Warrior Arts, headquartered in Richardson, Texas.

A.C.W.A. teaches reality-based self-defense, based on natural instinctive movements that are easily understood.

For more information, visit www.combativewarriorarts.com.

CHAPTER 2:
THE NEED FOR EFFECTIVE SELF-DEFENSE

BY LEONARDO LECHUGA
CHATSWORTH, GEORGIA

When I was growing up as a young kid I lived in an area where fighting was just a part of life. Fights were always happening and it was never anything structured or planned out, and I didn't consider it self-defense because it was survival. For me being able to fight and protect myself came from a place of necessity, and it wasn't until years later that I learned more about technique and ways to make myself even safer through more knowledge. I started training formally in Muay Thai and MMA, and from there I was hooked on learning more about realistic training and real-world self-defense.

Since I started my own training I've been on a mission to develop my own skills to the point of being able to train others. Now, as the owner of North Georgia Hayastan Martial Arts and Fitness in Dalton, Georgia, I use my skills to show people how they can become safer in their own lives. I'm now recognized as a person who can train individuals to protect themselves not just physically but mentally as well.

Self-Defense is a Polarizing Issue

Self-defense can be a very polarizing issue. As soon as people hear the term self-defense it can set off a range of emotions because the term means different things for different people. Some people may hear self-defense and immediately think of the ongoing debate about gun laws in our country, while others may think of personal protection of themselves and their loved ones. The truth is that self-defense is actually an extremely broad and encompassing idea, so in order for us to understand it we need to take a step back and realize what piece we're talking about.

For me the focus is on personal self-defense, meaning people doing what's necessary to keep themselves and their families safe and secure. Even broken down to this specificity there are still multiple layers to self-defense and we have to recognize that in order to learn to effectively defend ourselves. We need to understand the levels of self-defense and what those levels mean for our own reactions. For example, a person bumping you in line at the grocery store and then yelling in your face is an example of low level self-defense where you can diffuse a situation and move on using only verbal and mental skills. If that person then threatens you or your family, or actually assaults you, the level goes up and you need to be able to react appropriately. So while self-defense is a topic of debate, I think that having an understanding of what self-defense actually is may help educate people and lessen the disagreements out there.

Logistics of Realistic Training

The best self-defense training is training that is both realistic and effective. That being said, no one wants to risk injury to life and limb in order to learn how to be safe. This creates something of a delicate balance because if something is too safe then maybe it isn't realistic enough, but if something is too real then maybe it isn't safe. The solution as I see it is to build up to different levels of training. I don't expect new students to come in and jump into advanced training, but at the same time I have to have ways for those students to progress otherwise they won't grow and learn what they need to in order to adequately defend themselves.

One of the methods we use is training for different ranges of combat. If someone is at a distance and they start throwing things at you how do you react? What is the appropriate response? From there we close the distance a bit and learn how to react if someone is in closer range and we have to use hand to hand combat skills. Once those are learned we can progress to more advanced movements and then even onto weapons like bats or knives coming at us. Every range becomes a bit more serious and the threats more intense, but we build up to those things in ways that make sense so no one has to be afraid of being hurt because of taking on too much too soon.

Understanding What Works and What Doesn't

One of the biggest concerns I see with many other training centers is they only focus on certain aspects of self-defense. Focusing on only one area limits the person learning and puts them at a disadvantage when different situations arise. Some schools will only teach close range skills like punching and kicking, so what will the students do if their attacker is further away or has a weapon? Other schools only teach what to do if you're fighting on the ground, but what happens if there are multiple attackers kicking you in the body and head while you're rolling around with their friend? Another problem is schools that only teach partial attacks like scratching or eye gouging. This is a concern because these types of attacks aren't devastating enough to make a difference in a fight, and they also rely on fine motor skills which are extremely difficult for average individuals to use when their adrenaline is pumping.

As an example of how my methods are different, I teach about striking sensitive targets that are large enough to go for reliably. I also explain what to expect when these areas are attacked effectively. I'll tell someone to go after a person's ear while explaining that the ear is made up of cartilage and skin. I'll explain that biting into an ear is like biting into a tough steak, and to tear through it you have to bite hard and give a bit of a yank. I'm not teaching my students to scratch at someone's eyes or skin, I'm teaching them to go hard after sensitive areas because they're in a survival situation and they need to do whatever it takes to come home safe. What works is teaching people realistic and effective methods that will work regardless of the size of an attacker or a defender, and making sure the person defending themselves has the right mindset to do what's necessary.

How to Train the Mind

Probably the most important part of self-defense is the mental aspect. Getting into the right mindset and training ourselves to have the proper mentality can be challenging, but it's the foundation of everything else we do. The right mentality means being able to recognize the threat level in front of us and respond appropriately. Part of the problem is that we've become desensitized to things like conflict and foul language because we see it so often in movies and television shows. This is one of the main reasons we start off with verbal training before we even begin anything physical. I explain that if someone starts yelling at you and they're at a level 5 in their volume and demeanor, but you respond in a level 2, then you have a chance to bring them down as well. If they start at a 5 and then you match their 5, maybe they go up to an 8, and that's where things start to escalate quickly.

So we start off by learning verbal de-escalation tactics and being able to recognize the threat level and respond appropriately. After that we move on to physical aggression, and knowing how to react if a person comes at you. Do you need to grab them, take them to the ground and control them, or knock them out? It depends on the situation, but you've got to train your mind to be able to react to the situation you're in and act appropriately. The final piece of the training the minds is not only knowing when things need to escalate, but being ready to react. You have to be able to flip the switch mentally and know if you're in that situation where you have to rip someone's ear off. You have to be able to get yourself in the frame of mind where you're ready to do what you must in order to protect your life and the lives of your family members. It's not an easy thing to do, but it's a crucial piece to truly protecting yourself.

How Long Will It Take?

When people come to me looking to train, one of the things they commonly ask is how long the process will take. My response is to ask them if they're looking for a lesson or a lifestyle. I can teach a one day or a multi-day seminar and give people great core knowledge of basic self-defense skills and strategies. These things can be learned quickly and for many people it provides a level of knowledge far beyond anything they had previously. For some people they may be fine with just taking a lesson and moving on, but in order to really become proficient in self-defense it needs to be an ongoing process. A seminar simply isn't enough time to learn about the different scenarios and situations that could happen, nor is it enough time to learn the physical or mental skills that you must have to stay safe.

Another aspect of the process is being able to understand that not all attackers are the same. You may be dealing with someone who is just a run of the mill bully, and kicking them in the groin will end things quickly and efficiently. What if the person who's attacking you is a trained fighter, though? MMA fighters get hit in the groin all the time, and even if you land a well-placed kick it might not be enough to stop them – it might just make them angrier. So part of the process is recognizing the threat level of your attacker and how far you'll need to go, which is something that takes longer than a seminar to really understand.

Same Training for Everyone

When it comes to training in self-defense I don't think there should be any differentiation between training men and training women. In fact I think that doing this actually puts women in worse situations mentally because you're starting off with the assumption that she's weaker than a man. Why would you want to set a woman up for mental failure from the start by telling her that she isn't capable of training like a man? Look, it's not about brute strength all the time, a huge piece of self-defense if the force of will. It's the drive to survive, and that's what will make the difference in a self-defense situation.

Also, although women generally have smaller builds than men that isn't always the case. Would you tell a 120lb man that he has to train with the women because he's too small? Of course not, but what we can do is train people based on what works for them and what's natural. This concept pertains to gender, body type, and even age. Based on these variables there are certain things that may work better for some people than others, but my job as an instructor is to be able to train everyone. That might mean making certain accommodations, but it's important to focus on what a person *can* do instead of what they *can't*. Adjusting a technique so it's similar but different is ok if it feels more natural to a person, because that will mean they're more likely to use that technique. At the end of the day it's really up to the instructor to make sure everyone is receiving the same training, even if it means making those small adjustments so the students maximize their learning.

Final Advice

I hope this chapter has provided some insight about personal protection. My final piece of advice is that right now there is lots of talk about health and fitness, and I think that's really great. Take that to the next level, though, and try to incorporate self-defense into your fitness routine. Of course I think it would be great to take reality-based self-defense courses, but at the very least try out some kind of kickboxing or martial arts class. I encourage you to go beyond the treadmill and get into some kind of fitness routine where you can also enhance your self-defense skills. Good luck and good training.

Leonardo Lechuga started his career in mixed martial arts late in life but started with such dedication and determination that he quickly advanced into a high level competitor, trainer and coach.

Leonardo has trained with some of the world's best grapplers and trainers. He has trained with Gokor Chivichyan, Freddy George, Erik Paulson, Brenden Bohannon, Eric Turner, Eddie Bravo, Brandon McCaghren, and Calos Cummins as well as high level fighters like UFC Fighter Ovince Saint Preux, Former UFC Fighters Sevak Magakian and John Cofer, and numerous other high level fighters and trainers.

He has also trained several fighters to win Championships under several fight promotions as well as cornered numerous fighters and competitors with great success. He has also conducted several seminars for high school wrestling with an emphasis on Judo and Sambo for wrestling competition.

Leonardo has since taken on the role of Head Coach and Instructor at North Georgia Hayastan MMA Academy and teaches Grappling, Striking and Strength and Conditioning classes as well as conducts MMA Fight Camps and Fight Strategy Preparations.

For more information, visit www.teamhayastan.com.

CHAPTER 3:
DEALING WITH A CHANGING WORLD

BY TROY AUMAN
MANHATTAN, KANSAS

You are no longer sure if your environment is safe nowadays. You are no longer confident that when you plan to leave your residence you will return safely. You fear being snatched, stabbed, or kidnapped especially when you are in strange places. The result is you never get to enjoy life. You have created a bubble full of fears and doubts. Indeed, your world is no longer a safe place. You are governed by your own personal interests and you have to accept that you will be forever frustrated because you cannot make this world the safe place that you first thought it to be.

So, ask yourself: how can I make the most of my time on this planet and stay safe? One way to keep yourself safe from all this uncertainty is to learn how to protect your body through self-defense. For many, knowing various self-defense moves can contribute in a gargantuan manner to making this world a better place for yourself and your family.

A Self Defense Fanatic

Personally, I am a fanatic of self-defense. I have trained in traditional Taekwondo for decades and hold the rank of 6th degree black belt. I am also equipped with the strategies used in the traditional martial arts. Through the years I have introduced myself to the Israeli martial arts known as Krav Maga.

I will be very honest with all of you. I have not yet used self-defense to save my life and I think that is fortunate. Would you like to put your own life at risk just to be able to say that you have used your self-defense skills? Also, this is a clear manifestation that I have been so aware of my surroundings and situations at all times. I always carry myself in a certain way in order to be less likely attacked by any person around me.   Definitely, the way you carry yourself and being aware of your surroundings make a huge difference in regards to your safety as an individual.

Self-defense is like wearing a seatbelt. You wear a seatbelt not because you are planning on having an automobile accident. You buckle it for insurance. It is there just in case; it is your backup when you don't know what curve balls life is going to throw at you.

Learn Self-Defense

You should never be dependent upon other people especially when it comes to your own safety. The policemen around you are watching over not only you but the millions of other people walking around the planet. So, what should you do? You have to learn how to protect yourself. You can't sit back and wait for someone else to save you.

It is time to learn even the basic self-defense. You have to be your own first responder in all cases. You need to have a clear head; you need to have a good foundation of what to do to deal with the most difficult situation yourself; you need to be self-reliant rather than relying on somebody else.

Tae Kwon Do and Krav Maga

I have been sharing with people of Manhattan the two types of self-defense in which I specialize. I can say that I have been successful in hosting training programs, classes and seminars, and forging partnerships to really keep Manhattan safe. The two types of self-defense that I teach is Tae Kwon Do and Krav Maga.

Tae Kwon Do comes from Korea and is a traditional martial art with punches and kicks. You have seen it in the various "Karate Kid" movies. Many of you know about Tae Kwon Do so let me define the other one: Krav Maga.

Krav Maga originated in Israel where all of their citizens are obliged to serve and work in their army. Basically, Krav Maga is used in training the people who will soon work in the army. It includes hand-to-hand and self-defense tactical systems which have been proven effective in the army training. It is very gross motor skills oriented and it is very simple to learn which makes it so popular and effective in cases where a self-defense situation arises. Krav Maga indeed is known to be the ultimate human weapon. Strike, punch, the use of elbow and kick makes the great combination that will surely put you on the offensive and never in defense.

Someone attacks you so quickly; you need to flip the roll. You become the attacker and the attacker becomes the defender. As a result, in his brain, you are changing the dynamics of the fight to the point that you make him think he just picked the wrong person to attack. This is just one thing you can do if you learn how to use the Krav Maga. Though Krav Maga is more of being on the offensive it can also be considered self-defense because you are banking on saving yourself from an unfortunate scenario.

Learn Without Getting Hurt

You need to understand the art of self-defense. Most people think that during the training you need to get hurt in order to learn. I must tell you that this statement is a hoax. You can learn self-defense without getting hurt.

In reality, everything in the class is still a controlled setting. You will learn the aggressiveness outside our sessions. I have the rooms set up in a stressful environment and eventually you will forget the stress and just react. Then, when you experience the stress in outside world, your brain will work properly because it will think that you are still in a set-up room. You will be successful in doing all the stunts completely. You will think you are just in the class and not in an actual trembling scenario.

I will teach you to be very comfortable with the stunts. I usually start with the most basic stunts such as the strike and elbows, different kinds of hands strike and knees kick until you know how to develop power and use your body. Then you and I will start assuming scenarios in which you will apply those stunts. We will repeat it over and over again until you feel very comfortable with the execution of these stunts and you know how to put power to each stunt you make. When you are done with the basics we proceed to a more complex move--gun defense, knife defense, stick defense and, especially, the tactical aspects of training that are part of the Krav Maga.

Are We All Ready For Self-Defense Lessons?

You knew that it does not only involve the basic stunts but also the complex moves such as holding a firearm. Yet, not all people are ready to hold firearms and we are not going to force you to learn one. Besides, not all can acquire and afford guns, so why bother?

Instead, we are going to teach you the mental side of self-defense. Imagine you are trying to protect your home. You are with your family inside your peaceful home. Which side will they come from if there is an unnecessary circumstance? How will you defend yourself and your wife? How will you get your kids out of the scenario? You definitely need to create a space between the threat and your family. How will you do that? You need to prepare yourself for such a scenario. Paint a picture of what I asked you to imagine. If you are successful with this you can survive the scenario if it comes your way.

Self-Defense Is Not a Short Course

Seminars and classes regarding self-defense should not be treated as a short course. I cannot teach you everything. You need to continue to teach yourself to react to possible that might occur. You need regular, consistent training over an extended period of time to increase your potential of saving your life from an unwanted scenario.

Male and Female, Self-Defense is for Everyone

Both male and female are in need of learning self-defense. Regardless of your age, body build, and gender, you can do self-defense training by learning how to utilize your body when an unfortunate event begins to crumple your confidence. However, if given the choice, it is best to start learning self-defense as a child nine-years-old or younger. Though it will be a bit hard for him or her to cope with bigger bodies, learning self-defense at an early age is still a good investment alongside formal education.

Basically, the most important thing that you should know if you are interested in learning the self-defense is this: stress management. Here are additional key tips to help you safeguard yourself from any harsh scenarios:

- Beware of your environment and keep your head off your phone. You are not going to call anyone. You have to save yourself so live with it.
- Be conscientious of the places you are in. If you are traveling in strange places always observe your surroundings. Check for the places you can run to if anything goes bad and check your bag for things you can use for self-defense.
- Act accordingly for this will really place a great impact on attackers around you. Look smart and never look as if you are carrying billions behind your back. Walk with exuded confidence. Act as if you are familiar with the place. If you act accordingly attackers will think twice before they are going to attack you.

If you want to consult on how to become a good self-defender, you may check out our website: kansaskravmaga.com. Let us all be safe in a world full of "personal interests first" humanity.

Troy Auman is a 6th degree black belt, Internationally Certified Master Instructor with the American Taekwondo Association and Certified Instructor with Krav Maga Alliance. He has been training in martial arts since 1990 and has been running the Manhattan ATA since 1997.

He has also been a licensed school teacher with Manhattan Catholic Schools since 1999.

For more information, visit www.kansaskravmaga.com.

CHAPTER 4:
TRADITIONAL MARTIAL ARTS AND SELF-DEFENSE

BY TOM BURT
INDEPENDENCE, MISSOURI

Self-defense can be a hotly debated topic these days...especially in the martial arts world. People want to feel safe as they go about their daily lives and they often look to the martial arts to give them the skills to cope with a potentially dangerous encounter on the street. From seminars and workshops to full time martial arts schools there are a plethora of options available for someone looking to learn these skills and this can be a bit confusing as to which "style" to learn and what school to attend. As a martial arts instructor for the last 18 years I have worked with a variety of students from young children to older adults with the intention of teaching these techniques, not to promote violence, but to creatively manage conflict if and when it happens.

Personal Experience With Personal Protection.

In my opinion the ultimate goal of a martial artist is to avoid physical conflict and I am happy to say I have never had occasion to use my skills to protect myself...although I have used them to protect someone else.

Several years ago there were two men arguing outside a small shop a few doors down from my school. I had just ended my morning class so I was there with a couple of my students and we could hear the argument as our doors were open. The situation seemed to escalate as their voices became louder and insults started back and forth. I was not yet concerned as there was a woman there who seemed to know the two men and she was trying to calm them but we remained aware of what was going on to make sure nothing got out of hand. It wasn't until we heard the woman scream that we headed out the door toward them to find one man shoving the other into the store window and punching him. We pulled the aggressor off and restrained him on the ground while the woman called the authorities. When the police arrived we let them take over. I like to think we kept a bad situation from becoming something much worse where someone would have been severely injured.

There was another incident that happened one night at my school. I had taken the night off to spend with my family and left my lead instructor in charge. Some students from another school came by to challenge my students to fight. I had heard about things like this happening "back in the day" so I was surprised that this kind of thing could still happen. They were welcomed into the school but began challenging and taunting my students and staff. The lead instructor maintained respect by politely declining their challenge and asked them to leave the premises. When they realized they were getting nowhere with us they left all the while maintaining their taunts as they walked out the door. I was very proud of how my staff handled this as it could have erupted into a nasty situation.

Ultimately, I believe, it is awareness that is the most powerful self-defense weapon. Awareness of when to use physical skill, but more importantly when not to.

Awareness – Mental Self-Defense

When it comes to self-defense most people focus on learning the physical skills that can be used to counter a physical threat. While these skills are valuable, we need to understand that in our civilized culture the threat of physical violence is highly unlikely for most folks. However, all we have to do is browse the web and we will find story after story of assault, rape or murder. Just like car accidents happen all the time but the likelihood of getting in an accident is low for most people on a daily basis. As long as we are aware of our surroundings the probability of getting into a wreck is low.

Learning self-defense teaches us this kind of awareness, as well, so that we understand our environment and avoid situations where physical conflict may occur. Awareness teaches us to look for signs that people are angry or out of control so we can avoid them. We learn to do things like park our car as close as possible to the entrance of where we are going. When going out we are in a group of two or more. We search in and around our can before getting in. We learn to carry things like keys or bags in ways that can be used for protection. We walk with our head up and eyes looking around so we know where we are and who is nearby. Practicing this kind of mental self-defense can help avoid conflict most all of the time. So I like to think having physical self-defense skills is like having insurance. We hope we will never need it but we are sure glad we have it when we do. But if we practice mindful awareness the odds of having to use our "insurance" is greatly reduced.

What Is the Essence of Martial Arts Training?

Originally the martial arts were completely focused on staying alive in a physical conflict. But we need to understand that these "arts" were derived from the training given to soldiers for hand to hand conflict on the battlefield. With the development of "modern warfare" these arts became somewhat obsolete for military training but their essence and original purpose remained. When a martial artist devotes themselves to the long term development of these skills not only do they acquire the ability for self-defense but they improve their physical health through exercise and conditioning as well as their mental health by continuously learning and working on their character. So the martial arts become less about dealing with an attacker and are more geared toward improving one's own physical, mental and emotional well-being. Self-defense as 'health defense' you might say.

For example; statistics say heart disease is the leading cause of death in America. Yet our culture perpetuates the fast food lifestyle so that about 30% of adults and 17% of kids in the U.S. are overweight. Heart disease is preventable however, so part of teaching self-defense, I would think, should include instruction on proper diet and exercise.

Let's use depression as another example. The U.S. ranks 17th out of 156 nations regarding happiness with about 7% of adults suffering from depression. This trend is at an all-time high over the last 30 years. We continue to lose emotional connection with each other and our techy gadgets only serve to contribute to our somnambulistic coma so that we are only communicating with our children an average of only minutes per week! The media only makes things worse with messages of inadequacy unless we have this or buy that or make this much. We seem to be raising a generation of apathetic kids with low self-esteem. Is it any wonder that 1 out of every 100,000 kids commits suicide?

I think before we worry about the predator on the street we need to "defend" ourselves against laziness, poor diet and apathy.

The Broader Perspective

Ultimately the idea of training in the martial arts for self-defense comes down to improving self-confidence. We all want to feel good walking around in our own skin. There is no shortage of people in the world who know how to be violent without training. As a martial arts instructor my job is not to make people better at hurting others. The goal of the training is to strive for excellence. Doing our individual best with the tools we are given and then working toward improving that level of excellence over time. When we begin to feel good about what we can do then we can begin to feel good about who we are. This requires us to deal with a particular threat that all of us do encounter on a daily basis...FEAR.

There are two kinds of fear. Perceived fear and actual fear. Actual fear are things that we should be afraid of; healthy fears that keep us safe and are usually centered around avoiding physical injury. For example, I do not want to get in a car accident so I drive carefully when I am behind the wheel. We go to the basement when we hear storm sirens and do not pet strange animals to

44

avoid being bitten. Perceived fear, on the other hand, is being afraid of what we think **might** happen. For example, an attacker points a gun at me and I think he is going to kill me when, in fact, I cannot be certain this is true.

It is perceived fear that paralyzes us; that keeps us from taking action and it is this fear that we work to overcome in the martial arts.

Unfortunately, for the public in general, the martial arts have been relegated to either a children's activity or competitive sport fighting. This deters many adults from venturing into the practice. While martial arts are fantastic for kids and the skills of elite fighters are impressive the arts have evolved as a tool for becoming the best possible version of our selves we can become. A good martial arts program will balance quality self-defense training with personal philosophy all in an environment that encourages and nurtures the student.

Specifically with respect to what we do at AKKA; our practice focuses on a structured curriculum of self-defense based on the kinds of attacks likely to be used by attackers on the street. This includes defenses against punches, kicks, grabs, shoves or chokes as well as weapons like clubs, knives and guns. Techniques are practiced with partners so that in learning the defense mindset we also learn the attack mentality. Working slowly at first the goal is to be able to execute any technique, with controlled intensity, against a full force attack so that the defense is as effective as possible.

Is Attending a Self-Defense Seminar or Workshop Enough?

There are many good seminars out there with high quality information. However, the problem with a seminar is that there is no ongoing training. The student is left on their own to develop the skills they learned at the event. Without consistent practice, what was learned at the workshop will be useless if an attack ever happens.

The thing about self-defense is that it is an accident. What I mean is self-defense is what you do in response to an attack that comes without warning or provocation. Anything else is a fight and there is a big difference between the two technically and legally. So, in a certain sense, true self defense is an accident. So for the skills we learn to be of use to us they must be practiced over and over again in time to create "muscle memory" so that if an attack does come we execute the defense without even thinking about it. Most people who attend seminars do not follow up with this level of practice so joining a school that can perpetuate long term repetition of these skills, I think, would be the better choice.

Are There Age or Gender Specific Differences with Regard to Learning Self-Defense?

The main difference with respect to men vs. women in self-defense is the intention of the attacker. Predators will target women for different reasons than they will target men and their attacks will vary for women vs. men but the techniques used to deal with the actual attack are fairly universal across gender lines. In other words a man will more likely have to deal with empty handed or weapon strikes whereas a woman will more likely be grabbed. But the defense against a grab is the same whether it is a man or woman being grabbed. It is the situation that determines the technique, not the gender of the person being attacked.

Age, however, does play a larger role in learning self-defense. For example, children are not going to grasp the complex concepts of things like joint manipulation or nerve strikes. But they get it when you say block, kick and punch. So things for younger kids need to be kept at a basic level. As they get older and increase their mental development they can begin to understand more complex concepts and sophisticated motion. Adults, on the other hand, are more mentally and physically prepared so they can begin, at an earlier stage, to grasp the intricacies of the techniques we offer. Older adults are kind of in between as they can mentally grasp complex techniques but their physical abilities may limit them to basic techniques for them to be effective at self-defense.

What Are Some Things That Do Not Work or That Should Be Avoided When Seeking Self-Defense Training?

Don't be a "YouTube student". In other words, find a teacher and get good, quality training. Proper self-defense instruction involves training in a controlled environment with supervised instruction by a qualified teacher. The techniques work. A person's particular execution of the technique may not work so it is necessary to have a teacher to help improve your skill so it can be as effective as possible. As well, with this kind of training there is an inherent risk of injury so to minimize this risk it is best to seek out a good school with a qualified instructor.

Now, I am not one to question the efficacy of any particular art but there are some charlatans out there. With all of the hype and sensationalism in advertising out there it can be hard to know what is real self-defense and what is phony. Trust your gut and if it seems too good to be true it probably is. Do your homework. Ask questions. Watch several classes and go to several schools before you choose. Many people speak of a particular art being better than another. In my opinion there is no one art better than another. The one that is best for you is the one you like and that you are going to do; the rest is detail.

What Makes a Great Self-Defense Program?

I think there are three "kinds" of martial art schools: Fighting, competition and art schools. Fighting schools tend to be aggressive hard style arts that focus on dealing with fighting situations. Competition schools are more sport oriented with lots of trophies that focus on tournaments. Art schools are looking to teach an art form as a means of self-improvement. All of these "kinds" can be effective for learning self-defense. Keep looking until you find the program that is right for you. The art itself is secondary; as long as you give your best to the art you choose it will give its best to you.

Tom Burt is owner and chief instructor at AKKA Karate USA in Independence, MO.

With a background in Taekwondo and Tai Chi, Mr. Burt began his training in Chinese Kenpo at AKKA in 1995. As he advanced through the ranks he found he had a passion for teaching which led him to inherit his school in 2000. 2015 marks his 20th year studying the art and his 15th year as a school owner. He currently holds the rank of 5th Degree Black Belt.

Burt's teaching and training philosophy revolve around the core value of commitment. His goal is to inspire his students to aspire to be their best through martial arts training. Having been bullied himself he turned to martial arts to build self-confidence and now he works to pass on the benefits of training to his students. AKKA has been serving the eastern Kansas City area since 1986 and was recently awarded the Best Martial Arts Studio Award for Eastern Jackson County, MO.

Tom lives with his wife, Dee in Lee's Summit, MO with their son Joshua who is also a Black Belt at AKKA.

For more information visit www.independencemartialarts.com

CHAPTER 5:
SELF-DEFENSE VS. SPORT

BY VINCENT-MARCO DUCHETTA
ARCADIA, CALIFORNIA

I've been involved in martial arts for decades and have experienced all aspects ranging from realistic self-defense to sport style competition sparring and everything in between. I started out like lots of kids do, with my dad teaching me some boxing at home and basic stuff like how to make a fist and punch. As I got older I ended up getting into traditional martial arts because I was always big kid in class and other kids would come at me trying to fight. Martial arts was a way for me to learn how to defend myself and understand the difference between fighting for no reason and defending myself because I was in danger. Now I own and operate Ring of Fire Martial Arts Academy in Arcadia, California where I train students in a traditional style while focusing on real world application.

Importance of Self-Defense

A lot of people seem to think that training in personal self-defense, particularly hand-to-hand self-defense, isn't really necessary. In my experience I'd have to say that those people are absolutely incorrect. I don't advocate people learning how to fight for the sake of fighting, or to go out and use what they know to purposefully hurt or injure others. Self-defense isn't about that - it's about training for events that you hope will never actually happen, but being ready for them if they do. It's actually more about prevention and awareness than anything else, but you can't be aware of danger if you stick your head in the sand and pretend it doesn't exist. Instead I advocate that people learn about what dangers are out there and take the steps needed to be able to defend against those dangers if they're ever confronted with them.

Hand-to-hand self-defense in particular is important because it's the most common form of personal protection the average person will need in their regular life. Often times people will ask if they can just learn how to use a gun to defend themselves, and think that can be a final answer to any issues they have. I'm actually a big believer in firearms, but a gun is just another tool. I personally have handguns and rifles, but I've also got a family. An AR-15 rifle may be some terrific firepower, but if my kid is sleeping in the room across from me do I want to risk hitting them if the bullet goes through the wall? Of course not. Because I've taken the time to train myself in hand-to-hand combat I feel as though my skills are enough to protect myself in the home. So again, I do believe that guns and weapons have a place, and conceal carrying outside the home may be a viable option for some people, but a gun is just another tool and it's better to have more than one tool so you can choose the right one for the right job.

How to Effectively Train

As someone with expertise in a combination of traditional and real world self-defense I have firsthand experience in teaching the practical application of technique in day to day life without actually getting injured during training. In my martial art, Hapkido, there are lots of techniques that involve joint manipulation and twisting limbs in directions they're not designed to go. We don't just throw students in and have them start twisting each other's arms, though. There's a process to it, and one of the first steps is explaining the principles. The most fundamental principle is that we redirect energy, basically taking an attacker's momentum and using it against them. This principle is something we teach right away and use as a foundation for all of our techniques from beginner to advanced levels.

This is how training is done effectively. You can't expect to come into a class and be an expert, and an instructor shouldn't expect you to perform at high levels before you're ready. Effective training is training that builds a foundation, adds levels of difficulty as a student is ready, and provides realistic training. If all of these steps are taken, the end result is a student who becomes proficient in their self-defense techniques while also training their minds to perform in stressful real life scenarios.

Training for Everyone

An important aspect of self-defense training is that it can be done by anyone. In my life I've had the opportunity to train in a variety of different styles, but Hapkido is the one that has always stood out as the most comprehensive. Part of being so comprehensive is Hapkido's ability to allow anyone to train in it regardless of age or gender. If a person trains in kickboxing, for example, they can get really good at the techniques. They can learn the stances, the kicks, the punches, and become excellent. Now a person, man or woman, who uses these strikes against an opponent of similar size and build who doesn't have the same skillset will probably do very well defending themselves. What happens when a 120lb man or woman tries the same strike against a 300lb man? In scenarios like this size and weight will have an advantage.

In Hapkido weight isn't an advantage because we teach people to use an opponent's weight against them. This way we can show students, regardless of gender or size, that the techniques will work against opponents of similar size or even ones who outweigh them significantly. It's a style of self-defense that can be taught to anyone and isn't dependent on having the same strength or muscle mass as an opponent. This is also important when we look at ages. Because of the way Hapkido is designed I can teach students from very young to very old. Is a sixty-five year old man going to want to do a 360-degree jump spin kick? Of course not! But that person will absolutely be able to do the techniques we teach as realistic self-defense because we design the curriculum with real-life application in mind. We're not worried about scoring points for showy technique because we're teaching self-defense, not sport.

Self-Defense, Not Sport

In Hapkido we teach self-defense as opposed to sport fighting. We show our students how to defend themselves from start to finish, and to do just enough to get away safely. There are some martial arts out there that use pieces of Hapkido, but they teach their students to hit an attacker over and over as opposed to getting away quickly. I'm not teaching MMA fighters, here. If 120lb student Suzie is able to take an attacker down I don't want her standing there, resetting her stance, and getting ready for round two. As soon as she has the opportunity I want her taking off and getting to safety.

I want my students to have a clear goal in mind every time they train and anytime they have to use their skills in an altercation: get home safe. That's the only thing that matters to me and the only thing that should matter to them. It's not about submission, it's not about going multiple rounds to see who's on top – the only thing that matters is ending things as quickly as possible and getting home safe.

Another thing I want to touch on here that relates to this topic is the idea of being on the ground. Some self-defense styles actually teach students to go to the ground and defend themselves. We've also all heard the statistic that 70-80% of all fights end up on the ground, so I guess I can see where the mindset comes from. However, being on the ground in a fight is the worst place to be. When you're on the ground you can't see what's going on all around you and you're at a severe disadvantage if there are multiple attackers. You're limited to what you can do on the ground as far as techniques, and if an opening comes up to get away you've got the added step of getting up before you can take advantage of it. So while it may be true that a large number of fights end up on the ground I think the focus in ground training should be getting up as quickly as possible and staying on your feet.

The Adrenaline Dump

I've talked about some different situations that may come up, but one of the most important considerations in self-defense training is the adrenaline dump and understanding it. Some people have never experienced an adrenaline dump in a fight, but if you've ever been in an accident or other stressful situation you may recall a moment where everything slows down for you – that's the adrenaline dump. It's the body's process of actually slowing down your perception of time so that you can react. If you learn how to use it properly it can be an extremely effective tool in protecting yourself in any situation, from falling down stairs or being attacked on the street. The problem is it's impossible to fully control, and that's where training comes in. You can't control it, but if you understand it then you can use it to your advantage.

If you train in self-defense, putting yourself in realistic and stressful situations, then you'll be able to recognize the adrenaline dump and use it. You'll either get cloudy vision and feel like your legs weigh a thousand pounds, or you'll get crystal clear vision and experience clarity unlike anything else. You can't expect to get this type of control without training for it, though. In my facility, once students are ready, I throw them into intense situations in order to activate the adrenaline dump. It may be taking on multiple attackers, being backed against a wall, pinned against the ground, or other similar situations. You can't really ever control the adrenaline dump, but recognizing it and not being afraid of it is something we can train for.

Myths About Self-Defense

There are definitely myths out there about self-defense, and some of the myths are getting to the point of being seen as facts now.

One of the big ones is the idea that a person can go to a one or two-day seminar and come away with the knowledge they need to defend themselves in the real world. Don't get me wrong, I think seminars can be a great way for a person to get their feet wet and start learning about personal protection. The problem is that many seminars try to teach too much in too little time, and what happens is that people leave without really retaining anything meaningful. When I teach a seminar I typically keep it to four hours and no more than four techniques. This way of doing things allows for the limited information I give to sink in, and hopefully is enough to help a person protect him or herself. I truly believe that seminars can offer valuable information, and may be enough to save a person's life, but to really be proficient you need to take a full course.

Another myth I see often is how long a fight lasts. Fights don't usually happen the way you see them in movies, where there are two guys squaring off and trading blows for a few minutes. It's not like an MMA match where there are two trained fighters going at each other with rules and referees keeping things clean. In the real world fights are quick and they're dirty. More often than not what happens is one person attacks and the other person ends up cowering with their hands over their head waiting for it to be over. Knowing this, it becomes even more important to make the decision about which person you want to be – the one with skills or the one cowering on the ground hoping it ends soon. No one can make that decision for you except you, but once you decide to pursue training in personal protection you're on your way to keeping yourself and your loved ones safer.

Training is More Important Than Style

I think it's pretty obvious that I'm an advocate for Hapkido. I've had experience in a number of martial arts and I believe that Hapkido has the best chance at training people to defend themselves in real world situations. That being said, there are lots of other great styles out there and you have to find the one that works best for you. I think that an instructor and how they train their students plays a bigger role in self-defense than the style itself.

When you visit a school take the time to look around and ask questions. Check the instructor's credentials and try to find out if it's just a belt factory. Make sure the training being offered matches up with your goals, and don't change what you want out of training because someone tells you how much better their methods are. You'd be shocked at some of the false instructors I've come across who are taking people's money and instilling a false sense of security when they don't really know what they're doing. Making the decision to take the next step in learning to protect yourself is important, but take the time to make sure the training you're getting is the training you want and need.

Vincent-Marco Duchetta owns and operates Elite Youth Sports After School Program and Summer Camps at Ring of Fire Martial Arts Academy located in Arcadia, Ca. Mr. Duchetta has been helping kids in the San Gabriel Valley area of Southern California for over 20 years by teaching them the art of Hapkido. Mr. Duchetta has been an award winning speaker at many of the area schools and his Academy has won numerous people's choice awards locally for their ongoing support in the anti bullying and self defense programs they sponsor as well as teach at.

For more information, visit www.rofmaa.com.

CHAPTER 6:
FOUR STEPS TO SELF-DEFENSE

BY JIM HAMMONS
BROKEN ARROW, OKLAHOMA

When it comes to self-defense and personal protection, people as a rule don't realize there is a problem until there is actually...a problem. You don't always have a chance to see a bad situation coming until it's already happening. Of course we train to be more aware of situations before it gets to that point, but the reality is that most people are in the middle of a bad situation before they know it. At that point, you have to be trained, you have to have skills to go to that don't require thought. There's so many viewpoints and philosophies today about self-defense and personal protection, it seems never ending. As the the world around us has become more unstable, with incidents of violence rocking the news, I think the need for self-security and personal awareness seems to be finding a widespread preference of focus in modern society. That's happening as much for being proactive about dealing effectively with the unexpected as it is for people feeling insecure, maybe even more so.

Every incident screaming for our attention in the headlines appears to remind people about the need to acquire skills to protect yourself and your loved ones. Some consider self-defense purely a matter of security while some think it is a question of a mindset or a way of thinking required to keep you aware of all impending dangers. With about 40 years of martial arts training and teaching under my belt, and still going strong at Martial Arts Advantage, I have had the opportunity and honor of teaching these kinds of skills to all ages, lifestyles, and experience levels.

Personal Experiences

My story is much the same as any number of kids raised in poor neighborhoods. I endured bullying on a daily basis in my childhood. I was the child with tremendous health issues in a community filled with tensions and troubles, and hence was often picked on and harassed. The situation persisted even when I was older since I had trouble keeping up with the other kids. A slight build and being constantly sick and asthmatic made it difficult. The fact that I was the target for bullies inspired me to enroll in martial arts just to have the hope of getting through a day without being beat up. As I began to learn, I devoured every bit of knowledge I could get my hands on to enhance my self-defense skills. The training encompassed more than just physical defense as I learned tactics and strategies to neutralize situations with relative ease and without exposing myself to harm. Nonetheless, there were still a few instances where I had to apply physical combat skills to defend myself.

Is Self-Defense a Big Issue?

It's huge. There is a growing awareness in society about what self-defense entails, with a smaller percentage of people deeply understating its importance. We teach the concept that perception is reality to an individual. If you've never been bullied, attacked, or beaten then it's difficult to understand the reality of that experience. Think of this concept of deeper understanding by using swimming as an example. Swimming can be a fun leisure activity and a great way to spend some time with your friends. However, when you face danger in water, and you're literally in over your head, it becomes quickly apparent the ability to swim is far more than fun, it's a lifesaving skill. It is same way for self-defense when the need arises. Those that have yet to face being attacked or being in real life confrontations may not understand what can happen or how fast a dangerous situation can occur, and that if you don't have these skills, you or someone else may get hurt or worse. Living in the USA affords us more privileges than some other citizens do in more violent living conditions across the globe. You might live your entire life without seeing an occasion where you would truly have a need to defend your life, and that is our hope and prayer.

Being situationally aware is a critical skill to develop. It only takes a few moments to view your surroundings, understand the nature of what is going on around you and take note of where the exits are. My view on self-protection is wider than just deterring attacks. It involves being alert for fire risks, passing vehicles and any incident that can jeopardize one's safety.

Most people have minimized the idea of self-defense to the most fundamental aspects of the concept, fighting. Another concept we teach is to identify what type of situation you may face, then improving your response time to handle that type of situation. For instance, the average emergency response time for an active shooting rests between five and six minutes. Any training you receive needs to enhance your ability to survive for the first five to six minutes in such an environment. Within that window, the authorities are likely to secure the scene, keeping you safe for the rest of the evacuation process. Alternatively, in a face to face situation, if you can delay someone's full engagement by a few minutes, it is probably not going to occur. Self-protection is not always about the physical challenge, but being mentally and physically aware of the present situation and your options within those. It's vital information that far too few have been exposed to.

De-Escalation Versus Physical Skills in Self-Defense

When it comes to self-protection, different situations call for different strategies. For instance, about 80% of all sexual crimes occur with little or no violence. Your chances of avoiding becoming a victim improve statistically with any attempt to fight the perpetrators. What if you didn't know that? That knowledge alone could make the difference between an incident and a near miss.

When you become aware of an impending attack, or see someone approaching with ill intent, you should attempt to de-escalate the situation with things like facing the attacker with confidence, using the natural obstacles at your disposal to create a barrier between you and them, and using a strong commanding voice. By demonstrating confidence and showing that you are not an easy target, they are likely to simply disengage and look for an easier target. However, if you must engage physically GO FOR IT, don't give up and never quit!

I encourage regular self-defense training. Arming yourself with the knowledge and skill sets to neutralize dangers that can harm you or your loved ones is a choice, and a good one. A good training system will enable you to both understand the concepts and safely practice to develop those abilities and train you to act in the face of fear There could be times it will take doing all that you can do, just to keep yourself safe. Don't be the person who heard the message and ignored it, then needed it later.

The Ultimate Strategy to Self-Defense

Our training strategy entails a four-step process, regardless of age. With students ranging from kids to adults, we train different tactics to different age groups. The first step is to begin with avoidance. For instance, we teach kids to avoid playing with or being around kids who are bullies or who like to fight or be aggressive. Don't go into bad neighborhoods or places where gangs congregate - in other words, if you know it's a bad place or somewhere you know trouble happens, don't go there. For adults, it is living prudently and avoiding situations like places that promote prolonged drinking with people that lose sound judgement at the slightest provocation. Choose your friends wisely and, just like the kids, avoid situations and places you recognize are a hot bed for trouble.

The second stage is to get out of the situation. Walk or run, subtly or obviously, but if you realize you're in a bad situation and it's too late to avoid it, it's time to get out. This is where situational awareness being a habit becomes vital. If you know where you can go and you're aware of what's going around you, you can make good decisions about where and how to get out. If you're clueless, absorbed in your phone or unaware of your surroundings, or looking down when you're walking, those habits will work against you and you won't have an opportunity to utilize his second tactic.

If avoiding and getting out didn't work, the next stage is to use a "weapon of opportunity". You're still actively trying to avoid engagement at this stage, to discourage actual physical contact. For the kids, the weapon of opportunity is often to seek the teachers, friends and parents or guardians for support or to defuse the situation. If you can find something to hold during an attack, it might compel the opponent to leave you alone. The whole point of this tactic is to deter possible contact with the attacker.

When the first three fail, that can mean a confrontation has become inevitable. We recommend using avoidance, running, and weapon of opportunity for all ages, but if everything goes wrong, it's time to use physical skills. In modern society, you probably will find numerous instructors from the school of thought that a physical response is appropriate for every provocation. That simply is not fundamental to real self-defense and hence the need for avoidance to defuse the situation. That's the kind of thinking that leads to escalating a verbal argument into gun or knife confrontations. The best way to neutralize the situation is by avoiding or keeping calm and leaving without playing into the escalation that can happen. My duty is to ensure that all my trainees go home safe to their families.

Applying the Four-Step Strategy

Let's talk mindset when it comes to applying this strategy. It starts with living prudent lifestyles that lower exposure to dangerous conflicts. Secondly, if something comes up, there is no honor in fighting, live to fight another day and get out. If you cannot run or get away, the weapon of opportunity comes into play. Only as a last resort, use your defense tactics you've practiced and are trained in, and apply with rage and aggression. That way, you will get home safe and keep your loved ones from harm.

The Nature of Our Training

For realistic training, you need a competent instructor. There's plenty of so called "experts" who don't know what or how to teach, so you have to be careful about choosing who you train with. We teach a three-step process that aims at developing muscle memory, so if or when you have to use your skills, there's no thought required. In the midst of a confrontation, there is no time to try to remember what you learned that one time you took a class 5 years ago.

We move through the three steps of our teaching process by beginning with static training, followed by fluid drills, and completing with dynamic training scenarios. For example, static training involves learning the base skills and reactions without strong contact or resistance, where you learn how the skill works. You have to take time to understand the reasons why you do the skill the way we teach it. The next step is what I call fluid drills, and it involves actual encounters and drills with a little more pressure so you can practice in a controlled environment to adjust your stability and lock in more muscle memory. Finally, we use dynamic training scenarios which not only re-create real life situations where you might have to defend yourself, but also carefully but purposefully increase the stress and pressure in those scenarios so you learn to react properly even in an adrenaline filled, fast, dangerous situation. We use tools like practicing while physically fatigued, or in distractingly loud or chaotic surroundings, and in fight or flight modes but we do it in a safe and controlled environment so you can actually learn and practice. For example, we might work on how to respond to being attacked when you're on the ground or near ground level, like if you're changing a tire or gardening, by actually re-creating that scenario and practicing how to cope with an attack. What if it was multiple opponents or if a gun or knife was involved? As we create actual scenarios, we make ensuring the trainee's safety our priority.

Over the years I've noticed that people tend to underestimate the level of training they can achieve in two to three hours a week for several months, and they tend to overestimate what they can learn in a one-time four-hour seminar. We have a developed a instant gratification mentality in our society that encourages the idea that you can get things easily and without hard work, when in fact, real training and development of muscle memory involves work and repetition. It's true that unless you are attacked, self-defense training might be recreational. But, we have all seen the ever-increasing violence in the news, and if your life or your loved ones' is on the line, self-defense can become the one thing that stands between you and tragedy. That's how people ought to look at it as they protect their most valuable commodity-life.

Self-Defense Seminars

Self-defense seminars or workshops serve a few purposes, but they're quite different ones than the regular training we have been discussing. If you are already training physical skills, a seminar can take a specialty topic and take it to a whole new depth. When we are talking about the general public, I truly believe the purposes of a self-defense seminar are different.

In a few hours, you can teach a good amount of knowledge. You can expose someone to a thought process or training methodology. You can even take a skill or two and drill it to get some basic level of competence in relevant techniques you can use in the event of an attack. That's good! It's valuable! Yet, two of the best things that come out of our seminars is the increased level of confidence you get - which, in itself can prevent being attacked, and exposure to the type of training our regular classes provide. Perhaps you realize that the seminar gave you some awareness but cannot train you to attain expert proficiency. You can't get that from a short seminar or from YouTube.

Does the Four-Step Strategy Vary with Age or Gender?

No, the strategy stays the same. The tactics, however, are the part that can be different. Common situations for a 6-year-old and a teenager are quite different, as are those for healthy 25 year olds and a 75 year old with a cane. The ultimate goal of self-defense training is to create a way to protect one's life regardless of the age and gender.

For children, if they have been cornered into a physical confrontation, one thing we teach is the "air bender" technique. If you've ever seen the movie he takes both hands and pushes forcibly forward while making a powerful stance. This gives a child help to create a distance between them and an attacker by shoving, and then running to competent help. However, they need to learn the tactic in a way that keeps them safe in real action. On the other hand, if you are a parent accompanied by two kids, your tactics will be considerably different. If you are handling huge sums of money like a night deposit for your work, you need to learn knife and gun defense or understand how such situations present themselves. This is where training with real scenarios makes such a difference. As an instructor, I strive to learn and teach tactics that can work for the weakest and smallest of my students.

What Does Not Work?

There's so much bad information out there. One thing that comes to mind is instructing women to keep their keys between the fingers and punch an attacker with that hand. This risks breaking their fingers and isn't an effective technique. The long bones of the fingers are thin and hence likely to succumb to hard substances and pressure. It would be better to have one key, keep eyes up and move confidently than hold a set of keys in between your fingers.

What works? If an attacker demands your purse or wallet or other valuables, throw them in the opposite direction so you can run. Insured or not, it is ridiculous to put your life in danger over things you can buy. Your personal wellbeing is the most valuable thing that you own. Differentiate between bullies and people that are just rude by nature and actually being attacked. If someone says something bad about you or flips you off, that does not mean they are attacking you, and you need not respond as if they did.

Self-defense and personal protection are of vital importance today. Learning how to hone your instincts and skills in a safe environment is really critical. At the same time, you could definitely be trained and in great shape and still that doesn't guarantee you have perfect self-defense at all times. The reality is that we're here to stack the deck in your favor. It's about being proactive and taking steps to get knowledge and skills that make a real difference. In the end, remember that the only fight we never lose is the one we avoid.

Jim Hammons owns and operates Martial Arts Advantage in Broken Arrow, Oklahoma along with his wife Tracy.

Master Jim Hammons holds a 7th Degree Black Belt in Tae Kwon Do. He has been inducted into the World Martial Arts Hall of Fame, is a 3 time World Champion, and holds 16 National Champion titles. He has enjoyed teaching martial arts for over 30 years, and is a devoted husband and loving father of four. He is also a Financial Planner in South Tulsa.

For more information visit www.martialartsadvantage.net.

CHAPTER 7:
PERSONAL PROTECTION TAKES WORK

BY BRETT LECHTENBERG
SANDY, UTAH

I've been involved in martial arts and self-defense training for
nearly 40 years, but it wasn't until I got to college that I really
started focusing on my training and where I wanted to go with it. I
spent the first years of my training in a traditional martial arts
school, and have earned high-ranking black belts in Taekwondo
and Hapkido. Even though my instructor taught using a
traditional system he was very open-minded and actually
encouraged his students to add things to the art by exploring other
systems and techniques. His openness to other things is
something I've always respected and admired about him,
especially because his progressive attitude isn't one commonly
shared among traditional practitioners.

After training as an adult, my instructor encouraged me to open my own martial arts school. I decided that it was something I really wanted to do, but wasn't sure what I wanted to teach or even where I wanted to teach it. I didn't necessarily want to turn away from my instructor and his training, but I knew I wanted to do something I was passionate about. For me the most important aspect of training, above things like forms and sparring, was the realistic self-defense application of the techniques. Because of this I decided that I wanted to create something that was more unique to my own philosophies and personality, so I came to Sandy, Utah twenty years ago and opened Personal Mastery Martial Arts Center.

Throughout the time that I've been here I've been able to further refine my own beliefs about self-defense and have really taken the time to create programs that I feel have an important place in people's lives. One of the milestones that made a big difference in my training outlook was the birth of my son. It's amazing what having a child can do to your mindset, and for me it brought my focus more toward the training I can do to protect my family and my home. What I refer to as bodyguard science became something I'm very passionate about, and I've created programs and curriculum that revolve around family safety that I teach in order to help everyone protect the people they love and care about most in the world.

Importance of Personal Protection

I realize that there are people out there, perhaps even some who are reading this, who think that learning to protect themselves isn't practical or even relevant today. These people may have a mindset that learning personal protection isn't necessary because they trust that terrible things either won't happen to them or that if they do happen they'll be protected by law enforcement. While I respect that people are entitled to their own opinions, my opinion is that those people are living in denial.

One of the most common arguments against learning about personal protection is that "things like that don't happen here" or "that will never happen to me". Hopefully terrible things really don't happen to you or your loved ones, but how many people have car insurance and have never been in a serious accident? How many people have homeowner's insurance and have never had a house burn down? The answer is most of them, which is why insurance companies are able to make a profit. They charge their rates so people know they're protected in case something does happen, but for most people it never will. It's the same for learning how to protect yourself and your family – it's just another form of insurance. It's a level of peace of mind in knowing that if something ever were to happen you'd have the systems in place to take care of your family. In my opinion there's nothing in this world that gives the same level of confidence as knowing you can handle a crisis situation. Whether it's learning CPR, First Aid, or self-defense it's all about developing practical skills that can be used in case they're needed. You never want to have to use them, but you know you they're there.

The other argument against learning more about personal protection is the idea that the police or rescue workers are going to take care of you. I believe this mindset is absolute foolishness, especially if you look at the evidence of response time and how long typical incidents last. Average police response time in populated areas can range from three to seven minutes. Robberies and thefts can happen in less time than that. Even situations with active shooters typically happen very quickly, so a three-minute response time may be longer than you have. When you start talking five or seven minutes what do you think happens to your chances? What if you're in a more rural area and response times are even longer? That's why it's important to take the time and initiative to do things that may make your family safer instead of relying on law enforcement and other emergency services.

Can't I Just Use a Weapon?

This is another question that comes up a lot when we're talking about personal protection. Invariably someone will say that they carry a gun, a knife, pepper spray, etc. and can use that to defend themselves. I think that these things can have a use, but they shouldn't be a person's sole method of defense. Let's look at pepper spray as an example. For pepper spray to be effective an

80

attacker needs to be within about ten feet of you. If an attacker is ten feet away, they can close that distance within two to three seconds. Let's say that you manage to get your pepper spray out, open or uncap it for use, find and press the button while you're stressed about what's happening, and the unit doesn't malfunction. Even if all of this goes right it will still take seven to ten seconds for the spray to affect the attacker, during which time they can be on you pummeling and pounding. If they're on you there's also a chance of cross-contamination, meaning that your pepper spray is now hurting you as well.

I can offer similar explanations for using guns, knives, and tasers in a self-defense situation. Using any weapon is a lot to think about when you're body is pumping adrenaline and you're being attacked, and things happen in seconds not minutes. I think that with the right training there's a lot to be said for having some kind of weapon as a backup, but it shouldn't be something you rely and depend on in every circumstance. Carry the weapons if you want, but make sure you have more than one tool or strategy available to you.

How to Train

Once a person has made the decision to pursue personal protection training the next question they likely have is how can they train successfully in real world application without getting injured. The first things you need to learn are the concepts, like how to properly move and create distance. You have to learn about how to stay on target and hit your target even if it's moving or coming at you. It's about learning and understanding the basic concepts and principles of self-defense before getting into the more advanced areas, and that's how you stay safe once you do get to those more advanced scenarios. The problem is that many people don't want to take the time to work on this important foundation work, so they risk injury by starting in on the advanced stuff right away. The foundation is where everything is based from, so if you didn't learn how to make a fist properly then you're never going to be able to strike properly – it just keeps snowballing. It's a lot harder to unlearn a bad habit than it is to learn a good one.

Another key consideration for training is practice and role-playing. If someone only practices something they've learned a few times and then never go back to it then they haven't mastered it. They might get lucky and be able to defend themselves, but it's more likely that they'll freeze up and panic. Not being confident in something causes fear, that fear causes hesitation, and that hesitation causes even worse fears to come true. The way to overcome the fear is by practicing skills over and over, and then using those skills in role-playing scenarios that mirror real life as closely as possible. So training has to be consistent and it has to be realistic.

Can I Just Take a Seminar?

There's nothing wrong with taking a seminar. In fact, a seminar may be a great way to get your feet wet and make some decisions about how you want to pursue training and where you want to train. That being said, there are some things you should look for in a seminar before committing to it. One big issue I see in seminars that are offered is trying to cram too much information into a short time. Often a seminar host will try to give as much as they can, but too much information means nothing is retained. You may be able to perform skills at the seminar and feel great at the end, but what happens when you're put under stress? If you're attacked I can almost guarantee that you won't remember a move you practiced for twenty minutes a few months ago.

All skills are perishable and dissipate over time. It doesn't matter what it is, and technical skills dissipate faster than gross motor skills, but it happens to us all. For example I learned how to ride a bike when I was a kid and I still know how to do it. However, I was a lot better at riding a bike when I was fourteen than I am now because I did it every single day. Self-defense skills are the same – you have to practice repetitively over time to keep your skills sharp and ready. Again, taking a seminar may be a good start. It can let you get to know a facility, an instructor, a style, and see how you react to all of it. My recommendation would be to try and find an emergence course to really jumpstart your training, and from there decide how frequently you need to attend classes to become proficient at what you're learning. The answer may be different for different people, but ongoing and consistent training is the way to go.

Training for Men vs. Training for Women

In my facility I work with men, women, and children of all ages. People always seem curious about how the raining men and women is similar or different and that makes sense. For me I find that the best way to train is to have the same physical technique for both men and women, but the mental concepts are a taught a little differently. For men the mentality is often that with some training they'll be able to overpower an opponent fairly easily. They have visions of one-punch knockouts and ending fights without taking any damage, but the reality is that fights are dangerous and it's extremely rare that they happen that way. So men need to learn that they're not Superman, and have to sort of check their egos when they train.

Women, on the other hand, have the opposite problem. I don't mean to sound sexist, but in our society men and women are raised differently. What I find is that many times women come in and they are too nice, initially, to be aggressive and effectively defend themselves. They have the ability to do the same techniques as the men, but many times there's a mental block in the way. So what we do is help them to get into the right frame of mind. We have them visualize their child needing protection or something similar, and all of a sudden the fight comes out. We show them that what they're doing goes beyond the walls of the training room and can actually keep them or their family safe in the world.

When it comes to training men or women the most important thing is training the mind. We can work technique and repeat scenarios over and over, but without the right frame of mind it's not going to make a difference. So we give our students some rules. Rule number one is "give yourself permission to do whatever it takes to go home safe". Rule number two is "go home safe everyday". So not only do they have the rule of going home safe, but they also have the rule to do whatever it takes to make that happen. When we explain it this way and help shape their mindset the perspective changes quickly and dramatically, and that's where real self-defense starts happening. Once the mental edge is there a person can do any of the physical requirements.

What About Kids?

Kids need to be taught a little differently. The problem with kids is that they grow up hearing things like "don't fight, fighting is bad, you'll get in trouble, be the bigger person and walk away". The problem with this advice is the only ones who listen to it are the good kids, so they end up getting bullied or beat up because they're told they shouldn't be fighting. It happens a lot with kids who are black belts or who train in the martial arts. They have the skills to defend themselves, but because they're good kids who don't want to get in trouble they end up getting mentally or physically hurt because they don't stand up for themselves.

Kids don't necessarily need the rules about going home safe, and of course you don't have to scare a six year old into thinking that danger is around every corner. However, I think they should be taught that no one has the right to hurt them and that it's ok to use their skills if they need to. As much as I love teachers, I think that many times schools are part of the problem when it comes to this. So called "zero-tolerance" policies lead to good kids getting hurt because they don't want to be in trouble, but the reality is that getting in trouble isn't as bad as getting hurt mentally and physically by a bully who won't stop because they know their victim will just keep taking it. I teach my students that no one has the right to take away your ability to defend yourself, even your school. They need to understand the difference between self-defense, fighting, and bullying, and need to be taught what is appropriate behavior in different situations. Just like with adults, though, it comes down to practice and consistency.

Myths About Self-Defense

With so much information being available for people through various print and multimedia formats it can get difficult to filter the good from the bad. There are lots of myths about self-defense out there, and one of the most dangerous ones is the idea that there's one single solution to defend oneself. For some people they believe a single technique will work in all situations, like kicking someone in the groin. A groin kick can be effective, but this one single move is not enough to rely on. Similarly, people seem to think that carrying a firearm will be a 100% effective way to defend themselves.

The problem with this belief is that it discounts some pretty important considerations. One consideration is that a person who hasn't been trained properly and maintained that training simply won't be able to use any weapon effectively. Someone who doesn't practice proper form and technique when it comes to drawing, aiming, and firing a weapon isn't going to be able to perform in high stress situations. Additionally, safety procedures and protocols need to be practiced on a regular basis to ensure that a firearm isn't going to do more harm than good. Finally, people don't realize that in order to pull a trigger and fire a weapon aimed at another human being takes a certain way of thinking and many studies show that maybe 5% of the population is able to do it.

It All Comes Down to Training

I've gone through a lot of information in this chapter, but essentially what it boils down to is that if you really want to defend yourself and your loved ones you need to work at it. Taking a seminar to get your feet wet is a good first step, but you can't expect to take a day or two of training and rely on it when lives are on the line. In order for training to be effective when it matters it has to be consistent. One way to think of it is learning to drive. When you learn how to drive everybody has to obey the same traffic rules and regulations. There are maybe fifteen or twenty key concepts that you have to take into account when driving a car, and they're essentially the same for everyone. When it comes to driving, even once you get your license, it can take years to really be a "good" driver and be comfortable and confident behind the wheel.

In self-defense the other person isn't obeying the same rules as you. There are variables, concepts, techniques, and mental training that is required to be truly proficient in self-defense. So if it takes years to become a good driver, how can a person think they can learn how to practically defend themselves in a one or two day seminar? It just doesn't make sense. My advice is that once you've made the important decision to do what's needed in order to protect your life and the lives of your loved ones, take the time to find a training program that fits your personal philosophies and goals and commit to attending often enough and long enough to become proficient. Personal protection isn't easy, but if the time comes that you need it you'll be glad you put the effort in.

Brett Lechtenberg is Utah's Leading Expert on Personal Safety. His martial arts school, Personal Mastery Martial Arts, is focused on developing individuals through leadership, communications skills, confidence building, family protection, and much more.

Brett is the best-selling author of *The Anti Bully Program*, *The Anti-Cyber Bully Program*, *The Ultimate Travel Safety Program,* and *Protecting Your Castle.*

Brett continues his Personal Mastery Mission through his work with business owners and entrepreneurs to master their businesses and lives.

For more information visit www.brettlechtenberg.com.

CHAPTER 8:
KRAV MAGA RISING

BY MOLOTOV MITCHELL
RALEIGH, NORTH CAROLINA

Abductions, mass shootings, knife attacks, riots. These days, there is a growing, urgent need for personal protection skills. And as people search for the most effective ways to protect themselves and their loved ones, the Israeli hand-to-hand fighting system "Krav Maga" inevitably comes up. Krav Maga is recognized among military and police as a devastating and practical hand-to-hand fighting system. It's also well-known to many Hollywood actors, who swear by it as the best way to stay in shape. But Krav Maga is not as familiar to the American public as traditional martial arts like Tae Kwon Do and Karate, but that is changing. As a Black Belt Instructor who's been trained and certified in Israel, and the founder of both Triangle Krav Maga and the national Atlas Krav

Maga federation, it's my job to spread the good news of Krav Maga far and wide. So let's start at the beginning. What makes Krav Maga special and where did it come from?

Practical and Tactical

Krav Maga is an aggressive fighting system utilized by Israeli Defense Forces and Mossad. As the most brutal fighting style in the world, it has the reputation of being the fastest way to end a fight. Unlike conventional martial arts, our techniques are less flashy and more practical. We don't do jumping, spinning, upside down kicks, for example. We don't break boards or meditate. And that's why it's not a "martial art" per se; it's a *fighting system.* As we say at Atlas, Krav Maga is "all martial, no art". Krav Maga techniques often build on instinctive movements and reactions, making them easier to learn. Another aspect that sets our system apart is how we spend significant time addressing modern weapons and multiple attackers. Hostage defenses, knife defenses, even on-your-knees-with-a-gun-to-the-back-of-your-head execution defenses are a part of our system. Now, not all Krav schools are alike. But at Atlas Krav Maga, we put great emphasis on biomechanical expediency. In other words, we determine what move is statistically most likely to succeed, given the circumstances. What is the shortest distance from my striking tool to the target? Should I pluck with two hands for a quick grip or one after the other to generate more momentum? This "mathematical" approach dramatically improves the Kravist's chances of success in a violent conflict. And it's not just some theoretical style. Krav Maga is battle-proven. In fact, some of our Atlas shirts read, "Dropping Bombs since WW2!" And that's because Krav Maga is the only fighting system that was designed to destroy Nazis.

Dropping Bombs Since WW2

In the 1930's, as National Socialism was creeping across Europe, gangs of antisemites began terrorizing and killing Jewish people. In Czechoslovakia, a young Jewish man named Imi Lichtenfeld despised these terrorists and began planning to fight to the Nazi menace. As an accomplished boxer and wrestler, Imi had dozens of friends and students in the boxing and wrestling communities. After some of Imi's neighbors were beaten and murdered by Nazi gangs, the young athlete and his friends clashed with the Nazis in the streets of Bratislava, their home. Unfortunately, the Nazis beat the living daylights out of the brave Jewish fighters and it gave Imi pause. "How did this happen?" he wondered, after the fact. After all, his men were accomplished pugilists and grapplers. How did those untrained Nazi thugs hand their collective asses to them? Upon reflection, Imi's great revelation was profound and it's just as meaningful today as it was back then.

Imi realized that grappling and point-scored striking sports were not true forms of combat but mere imitations of the real thing. Wrestling, boxing, jujitsu, they all came pre-packaged with points, rules and regulations that hindered the practitioner in real world confrontations. I mean, it doesn't matter how great your rear naked choke is when two other attackers are playing football with your head, does it? It doesn't matter how well you can bob and weave when a Nazi produces a pipe and takes it to your kneecap. So, Imi went back to the drawing board and created a fighting system for the street environment, a style that dealt with weapons, multiple attackers and had no rules or limitations. After years of revisions and modifications, his new system became what we now know as "Krav Maga", which means "contact combat" in Hebrew. From then on, Imi and his Hebrew cohorts groin kicked and eye gouged the heck out of the goose-steppers wherever they found them. Krav Maga was officially on the map.

Years after his revolutionary acts against the National Socialists, Imi ended up in Israel, where Jewish settlers were fighting for their independence. At the time, Jewish families were routinely attacked by Islamic extremists with knives, sickles and the occasional firearm. He traveled all over, training neighborhoods and militia in the ways of his new "contact combat" system. As it had in Europe, Krav Maga proved very effective, this time against rabid jihadists a.k.a. the neighbors from Hell. And after Israel was established, the fledgling government honored Imi for his contribution by making Krav Maga the official fighting system of Israeli Defense Forces and Mossad, which it is to this day.

Krav Maga in Israel

Unlike most countries in the world, all Israeli citizens must serve in the military (barring special exemptions). That means that every adult in Israel has learned at least some level of Krav Maga, which may explain the country's dearth of person-to-person violence. Despite the headlines, I have never felt afraid or threatened on the streets of Israel. Everyone in Israel has a healthy respect for strangers. For example, let's say that you're a thief, standing in a Tel Aviv jewelry store. Before you even think of snatching a bag from that Israeli woman looking at some earrings, you have to assume that she knows Krav Maga and might put your head through the display case. But let's say she didn't. Maybe she's not Israeli, so you grab the purse anyway. Every other person in the store *also* knows Krav Maga and they will defend that woman. And even if you somehow manage to scrape your way out of the shop, everyone on the crowded street has trained in Krav Maga, as well! According to Robert Heinlein, "an armed society is a polite society". In terms of Krav Maga, Israel is predictably polite. Which reminds me of another country...

The Swiss Solution

In addition to hand-to-hand combat, Imi also trained with firearms. For that reason, I train students with firearms, too. While the government of Israel gives its people Krav Maga, the government of Switzerland gives its people...guns. And not just any guns. *Machine guns.* That's right, the Swiss government issues fully automatic rifles and thousands of rounds of ammunition to every household and at least once a year, citizens are required to train with them. The idea is that should enemy troops roll across their borders, the Swiss people can throw more than cuckoo clocks and chocolates at them. Instead of facing home after home, invaders would be facing fortress after fortress. Hoplophobes energetically contend that more guns equals more crime, but Switzerland disproves that theory. In fact, the gun crime is so low in Switzerland that they don't even bother recording it any more. The gun culture of Switzerland is responsible, it is safe and it protects its citizens. I believe that when we blend these two protective parts of Israeli and Swiss cultures, the hand and the gun (as Imi did), we can have the highest level of harmony and a healthy respect for our fellow man. I won't use the word "safety" here, because no one can guarantee your safety. But you *can* control your level of defensive power and that alone commands respect. And that's how you can, as Imi put it, "walk in peace".

Strength For Others

With Krav Maga, you can train to be a strong independent unit, capable of defending yourself, but I'd like to raise the bar. At Atlas Krav Maga, our motto is "Strength for Others". Simply protecting yourself just isn't good enough. Knowing that we often fall short of the goals we set, we don't set the bar at simply protecting your own body; we set the bar at being able to defend anyone within a ten-foot radius around us. Not only do we teach people how to keep a knife off of their own throats or defeat a choke, but also how them to protect people within arm's reach, their friends and family. If my goal is only to protect myself, I think that that's decidedly limited. And it may even be *selfish*. Shouldn't we invest in our community's well-being? I think that that's something that's really lacking in our society. We need to be thinking about others as much as we think about ourselves, if not more so. And if you learn to protect others, you will master personal self-defense along the way.

Train for the Mission

Students and instructors often ask what areas they should focus on: gun, gun defenses, counter abduction, home defense, etc. It all depends upon your mission. I have students who train specifically for a travel destination. They'll be in Bogota and they need some counter-abduction skills. I've had people bring me out to Cairo, because the Muslim Brotherhood was planning a coup and they needed gun and knife defenses. I once trained a woman who sold houses and ended up alone with strangers sometimes. Whatever your mission, tailor your training to it.

In 2012, "Handsome Scott" Woods and I created the Resist program, which covers active shooter training, escape and evasion, counter-assassination, and more. We've taught that to groups around the world, military units, police, etc. But for the average American, the average Joe who simply wants to protect themselves and their family, you have to train in hand-to-hand, and at least firearms basics.

Be the Weapon

I love to shoot. I'm a CCH instructor. I have a "Defender of Freedom" award from the NRA on my wall. I've got nothing but love for firearms. But unless you're engaging Taliban forces in Kandahar, hand-to-hand skills are far more important than your abilities with a firearm. To get the most bang for your buck (ha!), people should learn Krav Maga. You'll get the skills you need and along the way, you will get fit. Incidentally, getting fit is very important, because *fit people are hard to kill*. I have met more than a few gun fanatics that fall short of the word "fit". Bubble-bellied Bubbas love to say, "I don't need that *Jew Fu*." They gesture to the holstered .45 on their hip and mumble through their chewing tobacco, "I got my self-defense *right here*." Really? That's it? One of our t-shirts reads, "Atlas Krav Maga...because you eventually run out of bullets." What happens when you run out of ammo or your gun jams? What happens if the Enemy gets to you before you can reach that gun in time? What happens when you gas out after just 20 seconds because you haven't exercised in a decade and live off of a steady diet of chicken wings and Pepsi?

If a knife-wielding maniac charges me within 15 feet, I will *not* break leather. At that distance, under that duress, it's more likely that I would miss, shoot an innocent bystander or even shoot myself. But with trained fighting hands, you don't have to draw; they're *always* at the ready. And trained hands can do as much damage as any gun. Finally, unlike the exclusively deadly nature of gunplay, Krav Maga gives the practitioner a broad spectrum of violent options to choose from (up to and including lethal options). You can collapse the rapist's trachea or calmly restrain an inebriated brawler at the bar. With Krav Maga, you have *options*.

Allow me to put it another way. Don't count on a mechanical device to protect you. That's what *criminals* do and criminals are lazy. That's their deepest flaw, laziness. They don't want to wake up early and go in to work like the rest of us; they look for shortcuts in every part of their lives. This extends to their violent capabilities, as well. Criminals don't join a Krav Maga studio and train to master their bodies, because that's just too much work, right? They'd rather just get a gun. Well, after years of running ranges, I can tell you that devices fail all the time. And I certainly don't want that device to fail me when I need it most, when my life is on the line or worse, when the life of my child is on the line.

But don't get me wrong; when used properly, firearms are excellent force multipliers. For home protection, *guns are a must.* When you hear something go "bump" in the night, you need to be able to call the police, keep that gun on the door, and be ready to shoot. Even if you don't want a gun yourself, you should learn how firearms work. Let's say that a mass shooter rolls into your workplace, guns blazing. You need to understand why he stopped shooting. Is he reloading? If so, you attack. Or maybe he's heavily armored and his weapon is strapped to his body. You can't defeat him or take his gun away, so you have to eject the magazine and clear the chamber. You won't know how to do that without training. There has to be a balance.

I cannot stress this enough: don't put your trust in a weapon. *Become a weapon.*

Fit People are Hard to Kill

In Krav Maga training, we do a lot of isometrics, a lot of striking; people get fit rather quickly. In fact, some people train with us for the fitness component alone. There's a long list of celebrities who've used Krav Maga just to get in shape for films or even a wedding, like Russell Brand did. Angelina Jolie does it to stay fit and ferocious. Brendan Fraser took Krav Maga for his fight scenes in The Mummy films, etc. When you learn Krav Maga's valuable life-saving skills, your body is constantly changing for the better, and not just in your appearance. As you train, you learn to remain calm under duress. We call this "stress inoculation". And as you stress inoculate, your heart becomes more efficient, pumping more blood with less strain. Once upon a time, I caught a ricochet in the throat and nearly bled out. Thankfully, because of my training, I didn't panic. I was able to compress the wound and seek out medical attention before passing out. My body and mind were conditioned to be relaxed under duress. I didn't die, even though the doctors say that I should have.

Every year, people write or tell me in person about how they escaped a bad situation, survived an assassination attempt, used this technique to defend their family, etc. We have a long list of people who've used these techniques to survive, but there's an even longer list of people who say, "I have so much more confidence! I have so much more self-respect now that I'm fit! I just feel lighter, the way that I move in the world is so much freer!" *Krav Maga makes people feel great.* It gets those endorphins pumping, making you a happier person; you're more positive and you're definitely more assertive. You start standing up for yourself in ways that you hadn't before, because you've found a new kind of confidence. I like to say that Krav Maga makes us become our *best self.*

Never Stop Training

I love when people come to our seminars. They get loads of valuable information and training, but one seminar won't make you a warrior. You have to train what you've learned. Train, keep training and then train some more. The training never ends. About once a month, we hold RESIST seminars in North Carolina to keep people sharp. These seminars are extremely realistic. Our active shooter simulations are based on actual mass shootings and where they've taken place. We train in movie theaters, schools and offices. Students learn and train in those environments before the end, when they are tested. Active shooters come in, simulating different kinds of attack formations and students must do their best to "survive" the event. Students are pleasantly surprised when their new techniques work and they defeat the shooters. Others are very disappointed when they "die", as well. But that's also an important lesson, too. They learn what they need to work on.

Seminars are great, but never stop training. Even experienced Kravists must reject the lie that we've "made it" and don't need to train any more. False confidence is a killer, so train with knowledgeable instructors, absorb all you can and don't be discouraged when you fail. Remember that failure in combat is unacceptable, but it's okay to fail in the studio. That's where we learn, after all.

Training Women

Instructors ask me how I train women and the answer surprises some. Women need to be pushed as hard as men, if not harder. They are targeted by evil men from day one. Most often, they are at a physical disadvantage, as well. Women must train with men if they want to become effective Kravists. The best thing about Krav Maga is that size and strength don't matter nearly as much in the real world as they do in sports like wrestling or MMA. And why? Because no matter how much muscle a guy can pack on, his eyes will always be soft. His ears still peel off. His groin and trachea can't be strengthened to withstand striking. With soft targets like these, a woman can decimate an attacker twice her size without breaking a sweat. Remember, the goal is not to go 10 rounds with a "challenger" or score points. The goal is to maim or neutralize *Enemies* and get away as quickly as possible.

Some students have encountered traumatic events and are afraid to train, for fear of reliving a terrible experience. But there's significant evidence to support the idea that reliving traumatic experiences in a safe environment is an effective way to manage PTSD, so I encourage students to jump right in. It works wonders for trauma victims. One woman couldn't even leave her home after a vicious home invasion. I trained her privately at her home for a year, myself. During some techniques, she'd have to take a break to cry. It was difficult, but she never gave up, and eventually found herself training at our facility with guys twice her size. Instructors do women a disservice when they take it easier on them. Females aren't going to be attacked by a woman their size or smaller. Statistically, they will be face larger, stronger opponents. Women don't need false confidence. It's an instructor's duty to prepare them for the real thing.

Krav Maga for Kids

In America, most martial arts view kids as an easy audience. Just have them do some forms, give them some snacks and send them on their way. *But in Israel, teaching children is a great honor.* In fact, many schools will not even let you teach children until you've successfully trained adults for years! And I think the Israelites are onto something. When a child walks into a class to learn Krav Maga for the first time, that teacher is crystallizing our system in that child's mind, for the rest of their life. Teaching a child life-saving techniques carries great responsibility in many ways. Personally, I don't believe that the authentic, hardcore Krav Maga that we teach adults (eye strikes, joint attacks, bites, etc.) is appropriate for young children. With Atlas Krav Maga, I've created a modified kids curriculum called "Hero Academy". It still has all of the basics of Krav Maga, all the principles of Krav Maga, but it doesn't give them the more dangerous techniques too early. That being said, children can start learning Krav Maga as early as 4 years old. And by the time they're in their teens, they can be fully capable of protecting themselves and members of their family. *The earlier they learn, the better.*

For any parents reading this, it's also important to make sure that you put your kid into a responsible program. There are so-called Krav Maga programs out there where kids are sparring at 100% power, learning ultra-violent techniques and hurting each other. That's not healthy for kids, physically or mentally. Little ones need to learn and grow more gradually than adults. You can't just throw them in the deep end and say "Good luck, kid!" They are *the future,* after all. They should be handled with the utmost care.

Simple Math

As I mentioned earlier, Krav Maga is all about efficiency and what I call "high percentage techniques" or "HPT's". For example, imagine that you and a knife-wielding Enemy are facing each other and he stabs toward the center of your chest with his right hand. In Krav Maga, I would ask "what is the shortest distance from A to B or my defense to his offense?" Some martial arts will teach you to strike his right arm with your right hand. But in Krav Maga, we teach that the left hand should strike the Enemy's right wrist. Why? Because using my right hand against his right hand means that I have to reach all the way across my body to intercept the attack and that is a *long* distance. I've got a few scars on me from testing this theory, so I can tell you with full confidence that the right hand should not be your go-to defense against their right hand. The Krav Maga HPT is to strike his right wrist with my left wrist or forearm because it is the shortest distance from A to B. It's just simple math, and this mathematical efficiency is one of the things that makes Krav Maga unique.

Another difference is our *simplicity.* In Krav Maga, most of our self-defense techniques have only 2 or 3 steps. Any technique that requires more than four steps is just too complicated, in my opinion. Under duress, there's no way that you're going to remember a six-step defense against an Enemy swinging a bat at your head. Real world solutions need to be simple and they need to make sense. We never teach "horse stance", for example.

Spreading your legs leaves you extremely vulnerable, so I don't want to learn it.

The third thing that makes Krav Maga special is our *aggression*. We do not train to sit back and tentatively spar. We drive through the Enemy the first chance we get. That's not natural for most people. Aggression and the will to fight have to be developed. In Atlas Krav Maga, we say, "Be the Wedge" because we drive right through the Enemy. We don't stop or retreat. We plow through, even as their attacks glance off of us. When a wild haymaker comes flying in, we don't retreat or simply block, because that doesn't turn the tables on them. We *attack* the striking arm with the outer edge of our forearm while we simultaneously punch them in the face with the other fist. In Krav Maga, *even our defenses are attacks!* We don't have time to dance and spar with the bad guys. That's fine for Hollywood, but in the real world we want to neutralize the Enemy/Enemies as quickly as possible and get the heck out of there.

Stay Dangerous

A friend of mine told me about how he helped his son deal with his fear of the dark. Each night, his son would beg him not to turn off the lights because he thought "the monsters" would get him. After a while, the father started to get concerned. His son really needed to conquer this. So one night, he sat down with him and said, "Son, I know you're scared of monsters, but tonight we have to turn off the light." The boy knew this was coming eventually and replied, "Okay, Dad. You can turn off the light. But will you pray that Jesus keeps me safe from the monsters?" The father smiled and folded his hands to do so. But then he paused. He suddenly realized that he was about to send his son down a bad path that he would follow for the rest of his life. And so, he said "No, son. I won't pray that Jesus keeps you safe from the monsters. But I will pray that he makes you *dangerous*. So dangerous that no monster will ever want to touch you."

At Atlas Krav Maga, that's what we're all about. We don't promise that you'll be safe, because nobody can guarantee your safety. But what we can promise is that we will make you *dangerous*, so dangerous that no bad guy in the world would ever want to put his hands on you.

Dedicated to health and wellness, Molotov Mitchell serves on the Council for Physical Fitness in North Carolina (Wake).

An accomplished weapons trainer, he is liaised with the North Carolina Dept. of Justice as a Concealed Carry Firearms Instructor. In 2014, the National Rifle Association awarded him the title of 'Defender of Freedom'.

In 2011, he founded the award-winning Triangle Krav Maga chain of schools in North Carolina and later on, the RESIST program. He has taught Counter-abduction, E&E and self-defense courses in Egypt, Moldova and Israel. As a Krav Maga Black Belt, Counter-abduction specialist and defensive weapons designer (see patent-pending Hex Tool, Benthic Knife, etc.), Molotov brings a wide range of skills to Atlas Krav Maga.

For more information on Triangle Krav Maga, visit www.trianglekravmaga.com.

For more information on Atlas Krav Maga, visit www.atlaskravmaga.com.

YOUR NEXT STEP: DECISION AND ACTION

One of my favorite quotations from Anthony Robbins is the following:

"It is in our moments of decision that our destiny is shaped."

And what a powerful quotation that is. The roots of the word "decision" mean "to cut off." This says that when you or I make a decision about something, we cut off all other options.

After reading this book, or the chapters you read, what decision are *you* going to make about personal protection and self-defense?

Are you going to take a concealed carry course? Learn hand-to-hand self-defense? Attend a workshop?

Or something else?

Not only is making the *decision* important, but taking the *follow-up actions* is really what will make the difference in your life, and being able to protect yourself and your loved ones.

Our decisions shape our destiny. Our actions sculpt our lives.

Go out there and make magic happen for you and our world.

Made in the USA
Columbia, SC
05 April 2020

90826769R00065